Original title:
Peach Perfume

Author: Julian Prescott
ISBN HARDBACK: 978-1-80586-250-5
ISBN PAPERBACK: 978-1-80586-722-7

The Allure of Summer's Glow

In gardens bright where laughter flows,
The scents of joy begin to grow.
Bumbling bees in jolly flight,
Stumble 'round in pure delight.

With sun-kissed cheeks and playful grins,
A fruit parade where fun begins.
Each step a dance, a fragrant tease,
Nature's joke, oh how it frees!

Luminescent Petals and Warmth.

Beneath the sun, the petals sing,
Like confetti tossed on a swing.
Their laughter wafts through summer air,
A punchline wrapped with fragrant flair.

Sticky fingers and laughing shouts,
A game of chase, oh what a route!
The blossoms giggle as they bloom,
In a world that smells like sweet cartoon.

Sweet Nectar on the Breeze

A gentle breeze with mischief whirls,
As silly thoughts make laughter twirls.
Nectar drips from cheerful buds,
Creating giggles, golden floods.

With every sip a chuckle grows,
Delightful tastes that everyone knows.
A playful kiss from nature's hand,
Tickles the senses, oh so grand!

Blossoms in a Glass

In crystal cups, they twirl and sway,
Petals mock the serious day.
Bright hues dance like a lively show,
Making frowns just leap and go.

Pouring silliness, a glassful spree,
Each sip a burst of jubilee.
Fragrant fun, a merry blast,
A floral giggle, meant to last!

The Aroma of Autumn's Farewell

In the air, a scent so bright,
Leaves dance like they're feeling light.
Giggles weave through every breeze,
As squirrels chase their nutty keys.

Breezy whispers, a sweet charade,
Laughter hidden in the shade.
A whiff of joy, a citrus tease,
Who knew fall could smell like cheese?

Silken Notes of the Afternoon

A warm bouquet drifts through the park,
Where pigeons strut and leave their mark.
Tickles of sweet on the tip of the nose,
As ice cream drips and giggles rose.

Butterflies spin, like kids chase tails,
Every whiff's a tale that never fails.
A breeze that sings a quirky tune,
Afternoon sun, a goofy boon.

Fragrant Echoes of Love's Garden

Roses blush with a wink and a grin,
As bees buzz gossip, the games begin.
A fragrant swirl of silly sights,
Love blooms brightly, like colorful tights.

Tickling noses with every petal,
Cupid's clumsy, his aim not settled.
He trips on dreams, whirls in a spin,
In this garden, laughter must win.

A Symphony of Sweetness

A concerto of scents in a joyful pot,
Melodies mashing with all they've got.
Bubbles of laughter float to the skies,
With every note, a surprise flies.

Harmonies clash, like socks that don't match,
A symphony of flavors, what a catch!
Dancing through the air, oh what a prize,
Every giggle a note that never dies.

Orchard Secrets Unveiled

In the grove, secrets hide,
Juicy whispers all abide.
Breezes tickle, branches sway,
Bumbling bees are here to play.

Sunlight dances on the skin,
Drunk on nectar, let the fun begin.
Squirrels chatter, claiming space,
While I giggle, lost in grace.

Velvet Hues of Bloom

Petals blush in golden light,
Winking, daring, soft and bright.
Bumblebees don shiny suits,
Gathering sugar from the roots.

Daffodils join in the jest,
Tickling noses, they know best.
Nature's laughter fills the air,
Silly smells are everywhere.

Savoring the Golden Hour

Sunset drips like honey sweet,
Time for giggles, time for treats.
Laughter bubbles, time to play,
Chasing shadows till the day.

Fireflies flicker, join the dance,
Under stars, we take a chance.
With every scent, joy unfurl,
A fragrant giggle in the whirl.

Allure of Soft Blossom

Blossoms tease with soft allure,
This fragrant world, my heart's a tour.
Petal whispers, cheeky sighs,
Make me laugh, oh how time flies!

Butterflies, dressed up so fine,
Flutter past like winking wine.
Every branch, a joke to tell,
In this orchard, all is well.

Serenading Summer's Spirit

In a garden bloomed a scent so sweet,
Bees danced around, oh what a treat!
Wearing sandals, socks went astray,
Laughing loudly, we chased the day.

Lemonade spills, how did it happen?
A classic mix-up, we all start flappin'.
Rays of joy with a breeze so light,
Chasing shadows, we giggle in flight.

Silken Petals

A whiff of mischief floats through the air,
Tickles your nose, like a silly dare.
Flowers gossip in a giggly tone,
In this sweet chaos, we’re never alone.

A pie in the sky, or a cloud made of cake?
We run with delight, make no mistake!
Jokes in the breeze, laughter is spread,
Smiles with each step, life's joy widely bred.

Hues of Harvest

Ripe fruits laughing, oh what a sight,
Juicy jests, we munch in delight.
Bouncing in baskets, we leap and we roll,
Harvesting giggles, that's the goal!

Juggling the apples, fraught with despair,
One slips, and I'm in the air.
With grass stains and grins, we trip on our feet,
In this mad caper, life's rhythm is sweet.

The Essence of Sunshine

A splash of joy, a darting breeze,
Sun-kissed moments, oh, how they tease!
Mirth in the air, such a buzzing thrill,
Chasing the warmth, we’re drinking our fill.

Winks from the daisies, a jovial plot,
Under the sun, forget-me-nots rot.
With wigs made of flowers, we dance in a line,
Shiny and silly, everything's fine.

The Heartbeat of Blossoms

In a grove where laughter blooms,
Bees wear hats and hum their tunes.
Fragrant breezes tickle the nose,
While silly squirrels strike a pose.

The petals dance in playful ways,
As butterflies join in the sways.
Jasmine teasing with a wink,
Nature's party, don't you think?

Enchanted Whispers

A breeze that whispers silly things,
As garden gnomes sprout tiny wings.
The daisies giggle, dance in rows,
While dandelions wear bright bows.

Bumbles buzz with tales of plight,
Of missing socks, oh what a sight!
While tulips jiggle side to side,
In this fragrant joy, we abide.

Elusive Garden Alchemy

In pots where secrets brew and stir,
The herbs conspire without a blur.
Mint drinks tea with rosemary,
In laughter’s shade, quite merry!

The soil chuckles, cracks a joke,
While vines entwine like folks who smoke.
Tomatoes blush at silly scenes,
In this garden, nothing's mean!

The Soul of Summer Strolls

A stroll among the bright delight,
Where sunbeams play and shadows bite.
Chasing scents that lift the day,
We skip along, come what may.

Corny jokes from flowers burst,
In this realm, we quench our thirst.
With beaming smiles, we take our cue,
For silly moments, just for you!

The Air That Dances

In a breeze that tickles the nose,
Lurks a scent that giggles and glows.
Fragrance pranks with a wink and a tease,
Whispers of mischief float through the trees.

Like a jester on a sunny day,
It twirls around in a playful sway.
Each breath a chuckle, a frolic so sweet,
Nature's laughter with every heartbeat.

Hushed Elegance

Silken whispers on breezy trails,
Carry tales of mischievous gales.
In soft sighs, the aroma slips,
An elegant jest on nature's lips.

Dance of petals in a soft ballet,
Teasing noses in a charming play.
With a twinkle and a playful hum,
It's a giggle from blossoms, oh so fun!

Traces of a Forgotten Garden

In a garden where laughter was grown,
Mischief hides in each bloom and stone.
Unseen giggles leap from the ground,
Whispers of joy in the air abound.

A trail of joy, not too far away,
Where plants plot pranks in the warm sunray.
Every blossom with a secret to share,
Brings a smile and a twinkling flare.

Sun-Kissed Sensation

When the sun winks in playful delight,
Flavors of cheer burst into sight.
Bubbling giggles in every petal's hue,
Sun-kissed aromas whisper to you.

Join the laughter oozing from flowers,
Bouncing around those sunny hours.
When scents are cheeky, life feels grand,
With a fruity blast, nature's band.

Whispers in the Grove

In the orchard where the fruits collide,
A breeze of sweetness floats with pride.
The squirrels giggle in a silly race,
As bees do dance from place to place.

A plump round friend with a rosy glow,
Shares whispers of joy wherever we go.
The trees chuckle, their branches swing,
As laughter bursts from every spring.

Laughter of the Blossoms

In the springtime air, a silly cheer,
The blossoms whisper secrets near.
Petals twirl in a playful sway,
As they tease the wind throughout the day.

A friendly moth with polka-dot wings,
Flutters by, and the whole grove sings.
The sky is bright, the sun so bold,
In this garden, happiness unfolds.

A Garden's Sweet Embrace

Here in the garden, there's mischief afoot,
With giggles hiding where the flowers root.
A crafty cat with a knack for fun,
Leaps through petals, oh what a run!

The frogs are hosting a grand old show,
With tunes and rhythms that make hearts glow.
A chorus of laughter fills the space,
As blossoms bloom in a joyous race.

Elation in Air

Among the ferns, the laughter rolls,
As the sunshine tickles the garden souls.
A rabbit hops, then trips and falls,
While butterflies giggle, answering calls.

The breeze might giggle, no one can tell,
If the garden knows its own lively spell.
With every scent that floats along,
The world finds a reason to sing its song.

Nectar on the Wind

When summer breezes start to tease,
A whiff floats by, I laugh with ease.
Like candy shops that spin and twirl,
It tickles noses in a whirl.

Bees buzz madly, dancing about,
In fragrant fields, they spin and shout.
With sticky paws, they take a dive,
In blooms so bright, they seem alive.

The world becomes a playful game,
With every scent, it fans the flame.
I catch a whiff like a cheeky ghost,
And giggle at its sweet, sweet boast.

So here we are, with laughter strong,
As nectar slips, we hum along.
Let's frolic through this fragrant spree,
Where giggles mingle, wild and free.

Infusion of Joy

A splash of joy in every spritz,
A laugh so loud, it's hard to quit.
I tumble through the vibrant air,
And dance like nobody could care.

The garden plays a prank today,
With scents that lead the mind astray.
I close my eyes, the laughter flows,
In fruity dreams, anything goes.

Who knew aroma had such flair?
It tickles toes and ruffles hair.
A jogger stops to blow a kiss,
To scents so sweet, we can't dismiss.

In every nook, let joy collide,
With giggles bursting as our guide.
An infusion here, a sprinkle there,
We sip on laughter, breathe in air.

Delightful Echoes of Growth

The garden bursts, it laughs and sings,
With whispers of what joy can bring.
The flowers bloom in vibrant hues,
As butterflies don fragrant shoes.

Each petal holds a secret cheer,
A ticklish breeze is drawing near.
With every plant, there’s cause for glee,
We share the joy, just you and me.

The roots are solving giggle math,
While leaves engage in playful paths.
An echo spreads through every row,
For life's a joke, don't you know?

With every sprout, the fun multiplies,
As laughter dances 'neath the skies.
In every bloom, a story grows,
And tickles hearts wherever it goes.

Chasing the Scent of Happiness

In the breeze, there’s joy to chase,
With giggles hiding every place.
I run to catch that ticking sound,
Where every laugh and scent is found.

It skips and hops, just like a breeze,
Around the trees, it bends with ease.
Bouncing off leaves, a citrus play,
A wink of joy from day to day.

The world becomes a goofy chase,
As I collapse in wild embrace.
What’s this aroma? Lemon zest?
Or just my dreams that smell the best?

Let's join the chase with carefree hearts,
In fragrant fields where laughter starts.
For happiness is just a whiff,
A giggle shared, an easy gift.

Whirls of Citrus and Bliss

A blast of zesty cheer, oh what a tease,
The scent goes dancing, making all hearts sneeze.
It twirls and spins, like a giggling sprite,
A whiff and a laugh, oh what a delight!

In the garden of joy, where fruits wear a grin,
A splash of sunshine, it's a fruity spin.
With every sniff, my worries just flee,
Who knew joy could sprout from a tree?

Honeyed Secrets Beneath the Skin

A golden splash of sweetness, whispers in the air,
It tickles my nose, gives my eyes a flare.
Like bees in a frenzy, buzzing all around,
Unruly giggles in this scent I have found.

Underneath the layers, secrets do reside,
A little bottle of mischief, I can't let slide.
It wraps me up tightly, like a hug from a friend,
With every squeeze, the fun might never end!

Fragrant Allure of Forget-Me-Nots

Whiffs of laughter linger, soft yet bright,
In petals' embrace, secrets take flight.
Forget-me-nots chuckle, as breezes entwine,
A whiff of the past, sparkling like wine.

The fragrance dances by, like a sneaky tease,
It tugs at my memories, brings me to my knees.
With each little puff, I remember the grin,
A riot of joy, where the fun has been!

The Dance of Sweet Tropics

In a frolicsome breeze, oh what a show,
Tropical giggles, they put on a glow.
With twists and with swirls, they cause quite a stir,
I laugh at the fragrance that makes me concur!

Glistening sunshine, a carnival feast,
A bouquet of fun that never seems ceased.
The dance of the scents is a wild little game,
In this jungle of joy, nothing's quite the same!

Citrus Serenade at Dusk

In twilight's glow, the air's alive,
A scent escapes, our spirits thrive.
With each deep breath, the giggles rise,
We dance in zest beneath the skies.

Sweet drops of joy, in every sway,
Juicy laughter, come what may.
The breeze has tricks, oh what a tease,
It tickles noses, brings us to knees.

Lush

In gardens burst with fruit's delight,
We twirl and whirl, a silly sight.
A fragrance drips like melted gold,
And stories of mischief, we are told.

With each small whiff, our giggles grow,
Like frolicking sprites at the twilight show.
We prance and bounce, oh what a spree,
In scents of joy, we feel so free!

Sunlit Revelations

As sunbeams dance on playful cheeks,
The air is thick, allure it speaks.
A whiff so sweet, we can't contain,
We laugh so hard, it feels insane.

Our joyful hearts begin to race,
In fragrant bliss, we find our place.
Just like a pie, so full of fun,
We slice through laughter, one by one.

Essence of Joy in the Air

A puff of cheer drifts by our side,
It makes us grin, we cannot hide.
With every giggle, freshness blooms,
In scented rooms, we chase our looms.

Like bubbles popping in the sun,
Our souls are light, we jump and run.
This tangy tide, oh what a ride,
In every breath, we feel so wide!

Garden of Fragrant Whispers

In a patch of joy where laughter grows,
The perfume flirts, and everyone knows.
We prance around, like kids at play,
With scents that swirl and lead the way.

Each twist of breeze, a merry jest,
In nature's joke, we find our rest.
With every bloom, the laughter sings,
We're caught in joy, on fragrant wings!

Blossom’s Caress

In the breeze, a scent so sweet,
A burst of joy, no other can beat.
Bees buzzing 'round like they own the show,
Sniffing and dancing, enjoying the glow.

Petals chuckle as they sway in delight,
While squirrels perform their acrobatic flight.
A whiff of giggles in the air,
Who knew fresh blooms could play with flair?

Spring is here, and laughter’s loud,
Nature’s prankster, taking a bow.
With every breath, a chuckle ensues,
A mischievous bloom in vibrant hues.

So take a breath, and join the fun,
Nature’s laughter has just begun.
In this garden of scents, we dance,
With smiles blossoming in every chance.

Sweet Afternoon Melodies

In the park where giggles arise,
A burst of laughter, in a sunlit guise.
The air laced with joy, tickles the nose,
With each sweet note, the laughter grows.

Grasshoppers croon to a rhythm divine,
Creating a jam that's simply sublime.
As butterflies flutter, they join the tune,
Swaying and spinning 'neath the watchful moon.

A chorus of critters in playful disguise,
Singing sweet nothings and playful lies.
Nature's comedians, they take the stage,
Turning dull moments to giggles and rage.

So let your heart lift, let your spirit soar,
Join in the fun, we always want more.
In this sweet symphony, let's dance till we drop,
With laughter as our rhythm, we'll never stop!

Garden of Enchantment

In a garden where chuckles bloom,
Flowers giggle, dispelling all gloom.
Twirling daisies, a comical sight,
Stand tall and sway, as if in a fight.

The sun winks bright, and the breeze has a laugh,
With petals dancing like they're on a path.
Silly ants with their tiny parade,
Marching in time, their antics displayed.

The moon grins down, joining in jest,
As crickets play music, a nightly fest.
With each gentle breeze, the garden sings,
A chorus of joy that forever clings.

So wander in laughter, let worries fly,
In this magical garden, we'll dance and sigh.
With each blooming laugh, let the fun start,
In this enchanted realm, feel the joy in your heart.

Essence in Full Bloom

A splash of sunshine on a lazy day,
With giggles and scents that trickle and sway.
Butterflies plotting their playful schemes,
Leading us into a world full of dreams.

Every blossom whispers a punchline or two,
As they dance around, in bright shades and hue.
Witty vines twist in a humorous clench,
Making the garden their grandest wrench.

With every gust, a funny fragrance flies,
A tickle of laughter that never denies.
The earth chuckles softly beneath our feet,
As the universe sways to a comical beat.

So take a whiff of this blissful embrace,
Let laughter and joy bring smiles to your face.
In this fragrant escapade, we'll never frown,
With each bubbly moment, let's dance all around.

Golden Threads of Aroma

In the orchard, laughter flies,
Buzzing bees with silly ties,
Fruits swing low, like a good joke,
Nature's scent, a playful poke.

With a twist and a wiggly dance,
Fruit's allure, a daring chance,
Sticky fingers, giggles galore,
Who knew fragrance could be a score?

Cheeks blushing pink under the sun,
Silly faces, just having fun,
A waft of joy fills the air,
With every breath, a quirky dare.

Under trees, we sip and sway,
Scented dreams lead us astray,
With each chuckle, we unite,
In a fruity fog, pure delight.

Rapture of Nature's Touch

Sunshine spills, and giggles grow,
Fragrant frolics, to and fro,
Everyone's smiles, in a swirl,
A bloom of jokes to unfurl.

Swinging scents bring goofy grins,
Tickling nose and messy wins,
Hiccups from the bubbles we sip,
Nature's punchline on our lip.

In the garden, tricks abound,
Scented laughter all around,
Whiff of joy, so bright and clear,
With every breeze, we cheer and cheer.

The aroma guides our merry spree,
Plucking laughter from each tree,
In this realm of fragrant glee,
Who knew smells could set us free?

Dreamy Whispers of Youth

Childhood dreams float on the breeze,
Coaxing giggles with such ease,
Every whiff, a memory bright,
In the air, pure silly light.

Running fast, no time to tire,
Each sniff, ignites our inner fire,
With a fruity twist and a wink,
We laugh, and stop, and never think.

Nose in the flowers, oh what fun,
Life's little antics have just begun,
The scent surrounds, a playful tease,
Tickling senses like a gentle breeze.

Dancing in circles, losing track,
Who knew aromas would have our back?
With the sun setting low and the fun in sight,
In this fragrant world, everything's right.

Vibrations of a Warm Day

The sun blares down, a cheeky grin,
A warm hug, where laughs begin,
Breeze carries whispers, oh so light,
A day so bright, it's pure delight!

Squeezed from fruits, orbs of gold,
We weave a tale, sweet and bold,
Sticky hands and sugary fun,
Even the ants join in the run!

In the meadow, we chase and weave,
Each sweet tone, we can't believe,
Nature's giggle fills the air,
With every scent, we dance and share.

At dusk, we ponder one last cheer,
For this warm day that drew us near,
With laughter lingering, we'll decree,
Life's best moments come for free.

The Heart of Flora

In a garden, secrets bloom,
Little bees swing, zoom, zoom!
They buzz and twirl, what a sight,
Dancing flowers, pure delight.

A fruit with flair, sweet and bright,
Wearing scents, oh what a plight!
Sniffed by squirrels, giggling loud,
With every whiff, they feel so proud.

Tickling noses with their cheer,
Fluttering butterflies appear.
A whiff of joy, they glide along,
In this floral, fragrant song.

The petals wink, the critters grin,
A scent so strong, it pulls you in.
In Flora's heart, where joy's amassed,
A funny tale of scents amassed.

Luminous Elixir

Magic potions in the air,
Bottled giggles, scents to share.
Jars of laughter, shiny dreams,
A whiff of whimsy in the beams.

A laughing sun, with rays that tease,
Dripping sweetness on the breeze.
Every waft brings silly grins,
As bees bust out in funky spins.

Wobbly jellybeans abound,
Scented giggles all around.
Lemonade smiles, fuzzy limbs,
In this elixir, life just whims.

Glow of laughter, syrupy fun,
Chasing clouds until we run.
With every breach of scent we find,
A luminous joy that's one of a kind.

A Garden's Promise

In a patch of leafy greens,
Giggles bloom in sunny scenes.
Potpourri of silly stunts,
Seeds of humor, garden fronts.

Tiny critters planting glee,
Sprinkling joy with every spree.
Frogs in hats and mice in shoes,
Garden dreams, bizarre taboos.

Fluffy clouds, they're playing tag,
While cheeky daisies wink and brag.
Promising days of joyous play,
In this garden, come what may.

Chaos reigns with funny blooms,
Laughing winds in leafy rooms.
As petals dance, we can’t suppress,
The garden's promise is sheer success.

Touch of Citrus Dreams

A twist of zest in every laugh,
When life hands citrus, take a half.
With giggles gleaming in the sun,
A whiff of joy, oh what fun!

Tickling noses, citrus splash,
Pies of llamas, whimsy flash.
Oranges waltz with lemons bold,
Socks on cats, oh secrets told.

Puff pastry dreams and marmalade,
Hidden treasures, sweet charade.
The fruit performs its funny show,
In this dreamscape, laughter flows.

Sparkling juices, dance around,
A fruit parade without a sound.
With every squeeze, we find the cause,
A citrus touch, a round of applause!

Summer's Sweet Caress

In the garden where giggles bloom,
Sunshine dances, dispelling gloom.
Noses twitch at scents so sly,
Even bees break into a high-five.

Lemonade laughter fills the air,
As ants prance without a care.
Just one whiff, I’m in a daze,
Searching for that fruity haze.

Tomato wrestles with the vine,
When fruits get fresh, they feel divine.
Great grandpa’s toupee starts to sway,
As summer knows just how to play.

Whimsical breezes in my hair,
With each step, sweet moments flare.
Bring on the fun, let’s joyfully sprint,
Chasing flavors like a mischievous hint.

Gentle Hues in a Glass

Pour the sunshine in a cup,
Swirl and twirl, just can't get up.
Bubbles tickle as they shoot,
Sipping laughter, absolute fruit.

Rainbow splashes in the park,
Friends arrive just after dark.
Fruity glasses raised on high,
Competing giggles reach the sky.

Ice cubes dance a merry jig,
While laughter plays, and we all dig.
A tasty toast, forever bright,
Lift your spirits, hold on tight!

Who knew a drink could steal the show?
In this masterpiece, we all glow.
With gentle hues that never fade,
We sip on joy, never afraid.

Golden Hints of Eden

In a land where the sun takes a nap,
Fruits wear crowns, oh what a trap!
Bungling critters chase a dream,
Creating chaos, or so it seems.

A plump prize rolls down the hill,
Chasing it takes quite the skill.
Tickled toes on grassy floors,
Every tackle opens new doors.

Swollen cheeks and laughter shared,
Sunset paints all that we've dared.
Laughter echoes through the trees,
As nature hums a merry breeze.

In this Eden, gold and green,
Delights await, you know what I mean!
Every nibble brings out cheer,
Heaven’s secret, oh so near!

The Allure of Juicy Dawn

As dawn breaks with a silly grin,
Morning giggles about to begin.
Sunlight stretches, yawns so bright,
Whispers of joy take their flight.

Oh, the fruit basket's such a tease,
Who knew breakfast could be such a breeze?
Rolling out of bed with flair,
Chasing flavors, without a care.

Colorful dishes line the table,
Every bite tells a fable.
Slippery hands, don't drop a thing,
Let's dance with joy that breakfast brings!

As petals open and aromas burst,
I sip the dawn, quenching my thirst.
With smiles that chase the clouds away,
Each juicy moment here to stay.

The Scent of Late Afternoons

In fields where laughter dances free,
A hint of sweetness calls to me.
The bees are buzzing, quite absurd,
They think they're singers, but just blurred.

With giggles floating on the breeze,
The fruit trees sway with graceful ease.
I chased a squirrel, it stole my hat,
He wore it proudly, cheeky brat!

Beneath the sun, the shadows play,
A game of tag in bright array.
The air's a tickle, teasingly light,
Like socks on kittens, what a sight!

When evening falls, the sky's aglow,
A scent so silly begins to flow.
It's laughter wrapped in fruity bliss,
A memory you'll surely miss!

Sun-Kissed Wonder

On summer days when skies are blue,
I sniff the air, what's that, oh, boo?
It's not a cake or baked delight,
But something fruity taking flight!

My friend's a baker, oh what a tease,
He scents the kitchen with such ease.
But here outside, it's nature's game,
Whiffing quirks are all the same!

I tripped on daisies, did a spin,
The giggling flowers joined me in.
With every tumble, scents arise,
Like silly pranks beneath blue skies!

As fireflies dance through golden light,
The air's a riddle, full of fright.
But not of fear—of joy and cheer,
That wacky fragrance brings us near!

Hints of Golden Bliss

The sun beams down, a wink at me,
With fruity hints, a mystery.
A splash of color meets my nose,
Like jellybeans in rainbow rows!

My neighbor’s cat, a fluffy spy,
With fur so golden, oh my, my!
She lounges ‘neath the tree so grand,
Disguised as fruit—didn’t understand!

With every giggle, petals twirl,
The breeze is ticklish, what a whirl!
It whispers secrets, oh so sly,
Like sneaky whispers, “Try me, why?”

As dusk approaches, scents collide,
With playful shadows, side by side.
We’ll dance and smell the funny ways,
In whispering winds of fruity days!

Delicate Drizzle of Scent

A light drizzle from above descends,
Not rain, but fragrance, playful bends.
It's like a prank with nature's art,
I peek outside, it's quite the start!

The jester trees with wrinkled crowns,
Giggling softly while swaying down.
I wore a bloom like a proud king,
And danced about, oh what a fling!

The aromas leap like children play,
With every turn, they steal away.
I chase them 'round the garden's edge,
With wild delight, I'll set a pledge!

As evening settles, scents must fade,
But memories of laughter are laid.
For every breeze that comes and goes,
The silliness of scent still flows!

A Soft Embrace of Fruit

In a garden of giggles, I found my delight,
A fruity explosion that tickles the night.
With every sweet whiff, I dance in a swirl,
Wrapped in a fragrance that's sweeter than pearl.

The neighbors peek over, their noses all twitch,
Caught in the haze, oh what a rich hitch!
I wave with a grin, then I slip on a shoe,
Scent-surfing the breeze, with a fruity debut.

My cat turns her head, with a puzzled meow,
As if she knows secrets I can't even vow.
But who can resist such a charming bouquet,
When life hands you laughter in fragrant array?

So let's raise a glass, to the fruity affair,
To laughter and joy, wafting light in the air.
Let's waltz through this bliss, let our spirits take flight,
In this barrel of laughs, with aromas so bright!

Fragrant Delights of July

July brings a charm, wrapped in sunlight's embrace,
With scents that entice in a whimsical race.
A swirl of sweet nectar, it flirts with the bees,
As we dance with our shadows beneath sun-drenched trees.

The ice cream truck jingles, a comical sound,
While kids chase the melody, feet on the ground.
A splash of bright colors breaks over the green,
And the air is a carnival, fresh and serene.

We giggle and chuckle as flavors collide,
In a summer bouquet, where silliness hides.
The laughter of friends is the best kind of balm,
As we raise our cold drinks in a fragrant calm.

So let's toast to the fun, let the good times unfurl,
With each whiff that lingers, let joy give a twirl.
In this summer explosion of scents finely spun,
We'll savor the moment, till the day is done!

The Scent of Warmth and Wonder

In a land of sweet dreams, the aromas collide,
With chuckles and giggles, where laughter can slide.
A waft of pure mischief, it dances away,
A riddle of fragrance that comes out to play.

The sun gives a wink, and the breeze starts to hum,
While I chase down the scent like a bee or a drum.
Oh, the face that I make as I try to unmask,
This playful concoction, a fruity bold task!

Neighbors peek over, with a puzzled delight,
As I strike strange poses, oh what a sight!
I'll sprinkle the garden with humor so bright,
Turning scents into smiles, by the end of the night.

So join in the fun, with a laugh on the way,
A tangle of joy that will not fade away.
With fragrances tickling, let's swirl 'round and shout,
In this warm, wondrous scent, we'll dance it about!

Essence of Orchard Morning

In the orchard's embrace, the morning does sing,
With blossoms a-grinning, oh what joy they bring!
A pleasant aroma, it teases the air,
Like a sneak peek of laughter—do you dare to care?

A squirrel in the branches, a comic ballet,
As it leaps for the fruits in a plucky display.
No worries for weight, just a bounce and a flip,
In this radiant chaos, it takes a wild trip.

The breeze throws a party, uninvited but sweet,
As it tickles the cheeks, and dances on feet.
So let's join the fun, as the dawn's laughter swells,
In a riot of scents, where happiness dwells.

With joy on our lips and the world as our stage,
We'll twirl with these fragrances—life's amusing page!
In this orchard of giggles, we'll all have a thrill,
Where each whiff's a chuckle and time stands still!

Sun-Kissed Elixirs in the Heart

A splash of nectar on my nose,
A giggle escapes as it overflows.
Sticky fingers from fruity delight,
Chasing laughter into the night.

Bottles stacked high like towered dreams,
With each spray, a new silly scheme.
Sharing jokes as the sweet scent flies,
Creating a buzz that never dies.

In sunshine's glow, our woes disappear,
Each spritz a beacon, loud and clear.
Laughter erupts, a raucous cheer,
As fruity bliss draws everyone near.

So raise your glass, let joy ignite,
With citrus smiles, we take delight.
For every whiff brings a sunny laugh,
Together we dance on this fruity path.

Scented Adventures of Youth

In a garden where laughter blooms,
We weave through scents, dodging gloom.
With each step, a new mishap,
Slipping on dreams, the joy in a flap.

A whirling dance, we giggle and sway,
Sniffing our way through a sunny day.
Caught in a whirlwind of fruity fun,
Chasing sweet moments till we come undone.

We bottle our giggles, stash them away,
Each fragrant breath a wild ballet.
Squeezed-out laughter fills the air,
Fruity adventures we love to share.

Our youthful hearts, forever bold,
Once sweet and silly, now stories told.
In every scent, a tale to spin,
Where happiness starts, let the fun begin!

Memories Drifting on a Breeze

Whispers of sweetness float past my cheek,
Memories swell in the laughter we seek.
Like wind-chimes jingling under sun,
With a hint of chaos—oh, what fun!

A laugh like bubbles, they rise and burst,
In the warm air where friendships thirst.
We chase after scents, through grassy fields,
Where every adventure is joy revealed.

Drifting softly, that radiant air,
Laden with stories we long to share.
Each waft a promise, oh, come take a chance,
As nostalgia beckons us to dance.

Moments like candy, we savor the taste,
A sprinkle of sweetness, not a bit of waste.
In scents of laughter, let's drift and be free,
Wrapped in aromas of jubilant glee.

Floral Trails and Sun-Drenched Dreams

We're following trails of floral delight,
Where sunshine giggles dance pure and bright.
Like silly children lost in the haze,
Our spirits uplifted in fragrant plays.

With each step, we tumble and roll,
Bumbling through blossoms, heart and soul.
Silk petals tickle, a wacky embrace,
Sticky adventures, a joyous race.

Laughter spills like nectar, sweet,
In gardens of whimsy, we make our retreat.
As bees join our chorus, we sing along,
In this vibrant place, nothing feels wrong.

When the day dims, we'll not despair,
With floral dreams, we'll float in the air.
So chase those scents, let the good times beam,
Wrapped in enchantment, living the dream!

Fragrance of Dawn's Kiss

Morning sun with a giggle,
A sweet breeze starts to dance,
Flowers wink in their colors,
Spreading joy at every chance.

Bees buzzing like little cars,
Chasing scents so divine,
They trip over pollen jars,
In a world that feels just fine.

Chasing dreams on scented trails,
Bubbles of laughter rise,
Nature's wit never fails,
In this fragrant, sunny guise.

So come and take a whiff,
Of happiness in full bloom,
Where giggles form a tiff,
And joy dispels all gloom.

A Whisper of Transformation

In the garden of chuckles,
Where petals tell a tale,
A spritz of muted chuckles,
Turns the serious pale.

Bud to bloom, what a twist,
Perfumed with whimsy's grace,
Even the sun can't resist,
Joining in this joyful race.

Watch the plants wear their smiles,
Dancing in the warm breeze,
For miles upon silly miles,
Laughter flows with such ease.

Transforming the mundane scene,
With a splash of pure delight,
Like a playful, vivid dream,
Everything feels just right.

Laughter Encased in Bloom

In a patch of vibrant cheer,
Where giggles sprout like grass,
Petals clinking without fear,
Sipping joy from a glowing glass.

Daisies wearing silly hats,
Tiptoeing on lush green,
Bumblebees chat like sprats,
At a party, unseen.

Every scent a playful stitch,
Crafting smiles in the air,
A ticklish little glitch,
In this bouquet of flair.

Bursting forth with grinning blooms,
Laughter fills the sunny room,
Here friendships fragrance loom,
Even clouds can't help but zoom.

Scented Memories of Delight

In a whirlwind of sweet scents,
Memories puff like smoke,
Each breath a giggle-heist,
In the laughter we invoke.

Whiffs of childhood in the air,
Candy dreams and tree-climbs,
Jokes tangled in my hair,
Chasing time like nursery rhymes.

Every trail wrapped in glee,
Echoes of laughter roam,
Scented with pure jubilee,
Playing hide and seek at home.

With every pop of the day,
Memories bubble and bloom,
Casting troubles far away,
In a sweet-smelling room.

Elysian Fragrance

In a bottle, a sweet delight,
A whiff of sunshine, pure and bright.
Scented giggles float in the air,
Watch out, it's fruity—handle with care!

A dash of cream, a hint of cheer,
Spritz it on—no need to fear.
Friends may giggle, cats may purr,
Whirling joy, a fragrant blur!

Clouds of laughter, scented breeze,
Chasing joy with wondrous ease.
Dance around with fragrant flair,
Who knew happiness smelled like this, oh rare!

So here's to scents that make us grin,
A tickled nose, where fun begins.
Let the world catch a whiff of glee,
With each spritz, let's sip from mirth's cup, whee!

Lush Whispers

A fragrant tease in the morning light,
Whispers of orchards, sparkling bright.
Every spritz, a giggle blooms,
In a room like love, nothing looms.

The fox says, 'Hey, what's that scent?'
I laugh and tease, 'It's heaven-sent!'
A snack or two, maybe a pie,
Scented yum with a hint of sky.

Neighbors knock, they want a share,
'What's that fragrance? Can I get a pair?'
We laugh till our cheeks turn rosy red,
This merry scent messes with our head!

Floating whispers of fun in the breeze,
Spraying joy with utmost ease.
Oh, the bliss that scents can create,
In every drop, we celebrate!

Confections of the Orchard

Sugarplum dreams in a dainty spray,
A garden circus, come out and play!
Silly noses twitch with delight,
As aroma-filled jokes take flight.

Sticky fingers, giggles abound,
Chasing scents that swirl around.
A frisky fruit dance sweeping in,
Hop, skip, wiggle—it's time to begin!

Bumbles of bees join the fun,
Buzzing laughter in the warming sun.
Grab a spritz, let the mischief spread,
Sweet giggles are to be widely fed!

An orchard of laughs, a feast on the air,
With every puff, there's nothing to spare.
A fragrant delight, so wonderfully spun,
Nibbling joy? Now, that's how it's done!

Serenade of Soft Scents

A soft serenade, oh can you smell?
A symphony of sweetness, cast your spell.
Frolicking petals on a whimsical breeze,
Tickling noses, bringing us to our knees.

With a spritz, the world gets silly,
Transforming drab days into a frilly filly.
Socks and sandals, what a fun sight,
Dancing with scents through day and night!

Jokes bloom like flowers in heady tones,
Whimsical banter in fragrant zones.
Every laugh is a droplet of cheer,
Harnessing joy, it's the best time of year!

So listen, my friends, come take a whiff,
A joyful scent—oh what a gift!
Raise a glass to the laughter unplanned,
In this fragrant world, I truly stand!

The Language of Fragrance

In a world of scents and smells,
Where aromas weave their spells,
I sniffed a breeze, it danced with glee,
Said, "Why not smell like me?"

A whiff of laughter fills the air,
As friends exchange a fragrant dare,
One spritz here, a splash of fun,
Now we're two, instead of one!

The things we do for a good scent,
Like trailing petals, quite intent,
A dash of whimsy, nothing less,
As we enjoy our fragrant fest!

So let us blend with joy and cheer,
In this bouquet, we're all so dear,
The language here is quite absurd,
But laughter’s what we truly heard!

Tender Moments in Bloom

A whiff of sweetness, oh so sly,
Brought giggles as we walked by,
With every step, a funny twist,
What scent is that? We can't persist!

We danced around a garden fair,
Attempting to resist the air,
But oh! The smell made us all grin,
Who knew fresh blooms hid such a sin?

Together in a floral maze,
We snickered through that fragrant haze,
In every petal, joy was found,
With silly prances all around!

So here's to blooms that make us laugh,
In gardens bright, we cut our path,
Those tender moments, wild and free,
In laughter's scent, we love to be!

Sunlit Secrets

In sunlight's glow, we skip about,
Chasing scents, we laugh and shout,
A fragrant plume floats through the air,
Making us giggle beyond compare!

We stumbled on a hidden path,
Where scents ignited our heartfelt laugh,
With every step, a funny tale,
Whiff by whiff, we'd never fail!

Each twist and turn, a new surprise,
As we sniffed out hidden pies,
The way the breeze blew made us twirl,
In this sweet oddness, we unfurl!

So here's to chasing scents so bold,
In sunlight's warmth, joy does unfold,
With laughter shared and secrets sweet,
In every whiff, our hearts compete!

Nectar-Kissed Revelations

In the land of scents, we float along,
With nectar's kiss, we hum a song,
Each drop a giggle, a fragrant tease,
Bringing laughter, as light as breeze!

We sipped the air, a fizzy delight,
Making faces that felt just right,
The sweetness knocked us off our feet,
In this nose-fest, life's so sweet!

"Oh, what's that scent?" we jested loud,
As every whiff drew quite a crowd,
With fits of laughter, we declared,
Our noses are quite under-prepared!

So let's rejoice in scents that play,
As nectar leads us day by day,
With every splash and funny whim,
Life's too short, let joy not dim!

Fragrance of Summer's Embrace

A whiff of sunshine on my nose,
It tickles me right where it glows.
I chase a scent that makes me grin,
Like sweet confessions shared with kin.

A bounce in steps with every breeze,
My goodness, it brings me to my knees!
A fruity giggle dances near,
In summer's court, we shed a tear.

Oh, how the bees do love to buzz,
While I pretend to be all 'fuzz.'
With sticky fingers, joy we sow,
In this delight, we steal the show.

So let us laugh and take a swirl,
In this zany, fragrant world!
We'll sip on joy, we'll taste the sun,
With scents so sweet, we’ve just begun.

Aromas of a Sunlit Orchard

Through fields of laughter, we stride free,
With fragrant wafts that tease the bee.
They flit around without a care,
While I'm stuck here in my chair!

A juicy joke upon the vine,
I jest with fruit—my trusty line.
Each bloom a giggle, bright and bold,
In the orchard, tales unfold.

The sunlight winks, it knows my plight,
"Come, taste the joy, it feels just right!"
But here I sit, with nectar dreams,
And sticky situations, it seems.

With every breeze, my spirits soar,
And from those trees, I ask for more!
In this zany breeze of scents,
The orchard laughs, and so, it vents.

Essence of Juicy Dreams

At night my pillow starts to glow,
Of fruity dreams that overflow.
I giggle soft, I wake with zest,
In juicy thoughts, I feel the best.

The morning brings a bright surprise,
A scent so sweet, it meets my eyes.
It drags me out, I can't resist,
With every whiff, I clench my fist!

A splash of color, oh so bright,
I trip and tumble, what a sight!
To dance around on fragrant air,
With fifty grams of fruity flair.

So let's embrace this funny fate,
With giggles born from crave innate.
In every sip, each bouncy beam,
I'll toast to life, my juicy dream!

Whispering Petals

In gardens filled with whispered cheer,
The flowers blush; they know I'm here.
They mock my duck-like waddle stroll,
With fragrant giggles taking toll.

"Come dance with us!" the petals sing,
While I just grin and shake my thing.
A fragrance tickles, oh so sly,
I snort and laugh, then wave goodbye.

The breezes tease my frantic hair,
While scents encircle without care.
I stumble, tumble, in delight,
In this fragrant, floral fright.

So here I bask in joyful gleam,
Among these blooms, I chase my dream.
With whispers sweet, I shall embrace,
The humorous tales of fragrant grace.

Scents that Paint Sunsets

A waft of sweetness fills the air,
Like candy laughter, everywhere.
With every sniff, a giggle grows,
As fruity mischief subtly flows.

Sunsets blush with citrus cheer,
While squirrels dance, without a fear.
In gardens wild, scents collide,
Who needs perfume when you've got pride?

Morning dew like candy rain,
Leaves us laughing, feeling no pain.
In every bloom, a secret joke,
We smile together, then we poke.

When the night falls, scents still play,
Twilight giggles in their sway.
With silly dreams, we drift away,
In fragrant trails where fun holds sway.

Breezes of Tender Delights

A gentle breeze with giggles sways,
In every petal, fun displays.
Whispers tease of sugar high,
As butterflies giggle, flutter by.

The sun shines down like candy gold,
As our silly stories unfold.
Humor bloomed in every shake,
With each sweet scent, we smile, awake.

Crickets chirp a light refrain,
While flowers tease with their sweet gain.
Oh, what a riot, this fragrant spree,
Life’s a joke, and oh so free!

Dancing daisies, witty and spry,
Under the sky where laughter flies.
In breezes soft, our giggles rise,
A playful world in every guise.

Garden's Warm Embrace

In a garden bright, where giggles grow,
Fragrant whispers of fun do flow.
Pollen tickles with every sigh,
As flowers burst with humor high.

Sunflowers wink, mischievous sprites,
Tickling bees in playful flights.
The roses blush with each poke,
As laughter dances, lightly woke.

With a splash of color bursting free,
Each scent tells tales, wild as can be.
Under the sun, we laugh and play,
In this garden, joy leads the way.

A warm embrace, a fragrance bright,
In nature’s arms, we find delight.
With silly jokes in every breeze,
Life’s a circus, oh, so carefree!

A Symphony of Blooms

In fields of laughter, scents entwine,
A silly dance, a jester's line.
With every bloom, a joke is spun,
A symphony of laughter's fun.

Petals perform in colors bold,
As bees join in, so uncontrolled.
Their buzzing tune, a comic score,
In nature’s play, we crave for more.

Daffodils strut with goofy grace,
While daisies grin, a joyful face.
Their fragrant tales, like bubbles rise,
Bursting forth in silly surprise.

We sing along with fragrance sweet,
In this bloomin’ ballad, laughter’s beat.
Life’s a concert, scents in tune,
With every sprout, we laugh at noon.

Whispers of Blossom and Sun

In the orchard, bees do dance,
Chasing flowers in a trance.
Sunlight spills on golden skin,
Tickling noses, where to begin?

Silly scents that make us grin,
Like sweet giggles on the skin.
Winds carry laughter, light and free,
A fruity joke, come join the spree!

When apricots start to sway,
And all the odors laugh and play.
Nature's jest in every breeze,
Wrapped in sunshine, hearts at ease.

A whiff of fun on sunny days,
Ripening tricks in fragrant ways.
The world’s a silly, scented game,
With innocence as cute as its name.

Aromas of a Summer's Kiss

Beneath the sun, where laughter flies,
Fruit invites with goofy sighs.
A splash of zest, a twirl of cheer,
Whispers sweet, come gather near.

Ripe delights in every bite,
Silly squashes, oh, what a sight!
Chasing flavors on the ground,
Jolly scents that whirl around.

With every giggle, someone trips,
A peachy mishap on our lips.
The air is thick with joyful jest,
A fruity feast is what we quest.

Each fragrant breeze, a subtle tease,
With dance and hop, we find our ease.
In laughter's grip, we share a kiss,
In summer's arms, we find our bliss.

Nectar on the Breeze

In twilight's light, aromas soar,
Silly thoughts float to the floor.
The air is thick with fragrant giggles,
As blossoms sway and the heart wiggles.

A smell that tickles, a scent that plays,
Wandering through the golden rays.
Frolicking scents in purples and gold,
Mischievous scents, oh, so bold!

Aromatic rays that fly like kites,
Swaying softly, bringing delights.
Each breeze whispers silly delight,
A sweet serenade from day to night.

With laughter sprinkles, laughter bursts,
Bees join in with fruity flirts.
In every whiff, a story spun,
Life's a giggle under the sun.

Luscious Daydreams in Bloom

Daydreams drift on gentle air,
With flavors dancing everywhere.
A fruity lark, a scent so bold,
Teasing tales of ages old.

In gardens lush and laughter bright,
Whispers echo, hearts take flight.
Jovial breezes wrap us tight,
As blossoms chuckle through the night.

Each bubble of scent, a playful fling,
With happiness, the heart takes wing.
Sipping nectar from the sky,
Silly scents that make us cry!

With every whiff, a spark ignites,
Transported to those fragrant heights.
A melody of fun in bloom,
In nature's laugh, we dance and zoom.

www.ingramcontent.com/pod-product-compliance
Lightning Source LLC
Chambersburg PA
CBHW070309120526
44590CB00017B/2603
* 9 7 8 1 8 0 5 8 6 7 2 2 7 *